LICKING HITLER

Also by David Hare

PLENTY

FANSHEN

TEETH 'n' SMILES

KNUCKLE

SLAG

with Howard Brenton
BRASSNECK (Methuen)

Licking Hitler

A Film For Television by
DAVID HARE

FABER & FABER

London   Boston

First published in 1978
by Faber and Faber Limited
3 Queen Square London WC1N 3AU
Printed in Great Britain by
Lowe & Brydone Printers Limited
Thetford Norfolk

All rights reserved

© 1978 by David Hare

All rights whatsoever in this play are strictly reserved
and applications for permission to perform it must be
made in advance, before rehearsals begin, to Margaret
Ramsay Ltd, 14a Goodwin's Court, St Martin's Lane,
London WC2

Conditions of Sale

This book is sold subject to the condition that it shall
not, by way of trade or otherwise, be lent, re-sold,
hired out or otherwise circulated without the
publisher's prior consent in any form of binding or
cover other than that in which it is published and
without a similar condition including this condition
being imposed on the subsequent purchaser

British Library Cataloguing in Publication Data

Hare, David
Licking Hitler.
I. Title
822'.9'14   PR6058.A678L/

ISBN 0-571-11326-5

For REG

CHARACTERS

ANNA SEATON

ARCHIE MACLEAN

WILL LANGLEY

JOHN FENNEL

EILEEN GRAHAM

KARL

HERR JUNGKE

ALLARDYCE

LOTTERBY

LORD MINTON

Chauffeur, Maids, Sergeant, Soldiers, Naval Commander,
Engineers, Officers, Nurse, Voice of Narrator

Licking Hitler was first shown on BBC TV on 10th January 1978.
The cast was as follows:

ANNA SEATON	Kate Nelligan
ARCHIE MACLEAN	Bill Patterson
WILL LANGLEY	Hugh Fraser
JOHN FENNEL	Clive Revill
EILEEN GRAHAM	Brenda Fricker
KARL	Michael Mellinger
HERR JUNGKE	George Herbert
ALLARDYCE	Patrick Monckton
LOTTERBY	Jonathan Coy
Photography	Ken Morgan
Producer	David Rose
Director	David Hare

1. EXT. HOUSE. DAY

An English country house.   Perfect and undisturbed.
Large and set among woods.   The sun behind it in the sky.
Loudly a bird tweets.

2. EXT. DRIVE. DAY

A convoy of military vehicles comes noisily up the long
drive.

3. INT. CORRIDOR. DAY

A corridor inside the house.   At the end of the corridor
we can see through to the large hall where LANGLEY, a
uniformed army officer is standing.   The sound of the
convoy arriving.   An elderly CHAUFFEUR carries luggage
out of the house.   An even older MAID, in black and
white uniform, follows with more.   LOTTERBY, a young officer,
comes into the house, salutes, and begins reporting to
LANGLEY.   All the time the camera is tracking back,
drawn by the voice of ARCHIE MACLEAN.

ARCHIE: (V.O.) The question of Hess.

  (Pause)

  Nobody really believes that Hess flew to Britain on
  the Führer's instructions.   Hess flew to Britain for
  one simple reason; because he's a criminal lunatic.
  (The camera pans slowly round to a bare passage
  leading down to the servants' quarters.   A few

hunting and military pictures hang at random on the
cream walls. At the bottom of the passage the sun
shines brilliantly through the glass panes of the
closed door of the gun room, from which ARCHIE's
voice is coming.) Now what is frightening about Hess
is not what he has done. It is the fact he once
found his way so easily into Hitler's confidence.
As loyal Germans we have to face the fact that Adolph
Hitler chooses to surround himself with fools, arse-
lickers, time-servers, traitors, megalomaniacs . . .
and men who wish to rape their own mothers.

4. INT. GUN ROOM. DAY
ARCHIE MACLEAN is standing at one side of the room where
the shotguns are kept. It is mostly very dirty, full of
fishing rods, tennis racquets, golf clubs, mosquito nets,
sola topees, nails, hammers, saws, croquet mallets, polo
sticks, riding boots, skis, deerstalkers, wellingtons
and husky jackets. There is a table piled with cartridges
where EILEEN GRAHAM has cleared a space to take dictation.
She is about twenty-two, with very long legs and fashionably
long and wavy hair. She is efficient, self-contained,
lower middle class. ARCHIE is in his late twenties, but
already looks much more mature: squat, powerful, stocky,
a Clydesider with a very precise manner.

ARCHIE: God . . . God . . . when I think of the . . .
    (Pause. EILEEN catches up on her dictation, then
    looks away and out of the window, while ARCHIE
    searches for the right word.) . . . worms. When I
    think of the worms, when I think of the cheapjacks,
    when I think of the human excrement that is even now

clogging up the innermost councils of the Reich, when
I think how badly divided our leaders are, how grossly
they have miscalculated, how the pygmies scratch and
. . . *(Pause. Action again suspended.)* . . . jostle.
Jostle round the Führer's teats, how the greybeard
eunuchs and slug-like parvenues congest and clot the
bloodstream of the nation, then I cry . . . Lord I
cry for Germany. *(He turns and looks at EILEEN still
thinking. She looks up. Then he waves a hand.)*
Something like that.

5. EXT. COUNTRY LANE. DAY
*Country lane in spring. A young girl of nineteen,
struggling along the road, which is deserted, carrying two
heavy suitcases which she has to put down every fifty
yards. Her hair falls in front of her face. She is thin
and very tired. ANNA.*

6. INT. HALL. DAY
*A large hall with a fine staircase. The front doors of the
house have been flung open and opposite them the military
vehicles are now parked and are being unloaded by
SOLDIERS under the direction of the SERGEANT. They are
taking off office equipment which they now bring into
the house. Also waiting outside is an old Rolls-Royce.
At the very centre of the hall LORD MINTON is sitting on
his suitcase. He has a stick, a big black coat and is
very old and ill. Around him, and taking no notice,
SOLDIERS carry filing cabinets and wireless equipment
through the hall and off down the corridor.
LANGLEY comes down the staircase. We see him to be in
his thirties, thin, boney, with sleeked-down black hair*

and a very dry edge to his manner. *ALLARDYCE, a young engineer, approaches him, carrying a green telephone.*

ALLARDYCE: The green line, sir, anywhere in particular?

LANGLEY: Best place is my study. I'll show you where that is.

(ARCHIE is standing in his shirt-sleeves at the end of the corridor watching the arrivals. LANGLEY gestures to him.)

Archie, can you . . .

(LANGLEY nods, then disappears with ALLARDYCE and the telephone equipment. ARCHIE looks across at the CHAUFFEUR who is coming back from the car.)

ARCHIE: Is he ready?

(The CHAUFFEUR looks down at LORD MINTON and asks him a question in deaf and dumb language. LORD MINTON replies vociferously, then turns to ARCHIE. Gets up. He smiles and gestures wonderingly round the magnificent house. Then shrugs. ARCHIE hands him his cane and gloves.)

7. EXT. STEPS OF THE HOUSE. DAY

ARCHIE shakes MINTON's hand and shouts at him.

ARCHIE: Very kind. Of you. To lend us. Your place.

(MINTON turns and gets into the car, the door of which is held open for him by his CHAUFFEUR.)

Tell him we appreciate his sacrifice. Having to spend the rest of the war in that squalid wee single end in Eaton Square.

(The CHAUFFEUR smiles thinly as he closes the door, and goes round to drive away. ANNA arrives just in time to hear ARCHIE as he waves from the steps.)

That's right Minton, you bugger off.

(ANNA looks up at him.)

ANNA: Is this Wendlesham?

ARCHIE: You were due yesterday.

ANNA: The train . . . it stopped for the night outside
  Aylesbury. Nobody knew why.
  *(But ARCHIE has already turned to LOTTERBY, who is
  carrying a huge photograph of Goebbels into the house.
  ARCHIE seizes it.)*
  And it's taken all day just to get . . .

LOTTERBY: Goebbels for you Sir.

  (ARCHIE smiles and goes into the house.)

ARCHIE: We'll hang him in the study. Is that not what
  people do?

8. INT. HALL. DAY

*ARCHIE passes quickly through with LOTTERBY carrying the
portrait of Goebbels.*

ARCHIE: Look at the face. Extraordinary face. The lips.
  *(They go off down the corridor. ANNA follows in
  through the door and looks round the hall which has
  suddently emptied. She puts her bags down, looks
  round. Sudden quiet.)*

9. EXT. DRIVE. DAY

The military convoy disappears down the drive.

10. GUN ROOM. DAY

*As before except now at the centre of the clutter is the
large and magnificent portrait of Goebbels. ARCHIE is
standing at the window. It is darkening outside. EILEEN
is sitting at the desk reading back typed dictation.*

EILEEN: The question of Hess, stop. Nobody believes that

15

Hess came to Britain on the Führer's instructions,
stop. Hess flew to Britain for one simple reason, colon.
Because he's a criminal lunatic, stop.

*(ANNA is standing at the door. She has taken her coat
off and has tidied up. She carries a huge volume under
her arm. EILEEN stops reading. ARCHIE turns.)*

ARCHIE: I take it you've signed the Act. *(ANNA nods.)*
Sit down. *(ANNA sits on a wooden chair among the tennis
racquets.)* Ihr Deutsch soll ausgezeichnet sein.

ANNA: Ja. Das war ja einfach für mich.

ARCHIE: Where did you learn?

ANNA: My family . . . my cousin was married to a German.
I spent my summers in Oberwesel. They had a schloss
on the Rhine.

ARCHIE: Who vetted you?

ANNA: Naval Intelligence. My uncle is Second Sea Lord at
the Admiralty . . . .

ARCHIE: I see.

ANNA: I also have a cousin who's high up in . . .

ARCHIE: Och yes, I can imagine.

(There is a pause. ARCHIE looks at ANNA.)
Well there's nothing for you yet. But we do need
somebody to make the tea.

11. INT. KITCHEN. EVENING

*A large bare room with a gas range. The only provisions
in view are a packet of tea, a packet of sugar and a
bottle of milk. ANNA comes in, looks around, then takes
a saucepan over to the tap. We can hear EILEEN in the
distance repeating the Hess speech. ANNA pauses uncertainly
at the tap, then turns back, takes a decision. She
confidently empties the whole packet of tea into the*
16

saucepan and pours onto it a good hard gush of cold water.
She then puts the pan onto the gas and lights it.

12. INT. CORRIDOR. EVENING
Empty. Gun room door open.
ARCHIE: (V.O.) I'll do the blackout, it's a'right.
   (EILEEN appears from the gun room, looks puzzled down
   the corridor, then goes one door down to the kitchen.
   Goes in.)

13. INT. KITCHEN. EVENING
The tea is now boiling, ANNA is staring at it. She looks
up at EILEEN as soon as she comes in. EILEEN at once takes
it off the stove, amazed, and looks at the empty packet.
EILEEN: That's a week's ration.
ANNA: I've never had to. *(She is beginning to cry.)*
EILEEN: No
ANNA: Just can't.

14. INT. BEDROOM. NIGHT
A darkened room, plain, once a servant's bedroom. An iron
bed. ANNA lying awake in the dark. Then quietly she slips
the covers off and runs across to her suitcase at the far
side of the room. Takes out her battered, yellowing teddy
bear. Returns to bed with him. Stops in front of the bed.
ANNA: Which side do you want?

15. INT. DRAWING ROOM. DAY
A magnificent yellow room. High windows. Bright daylight.
Armchairs and sofas. Superb full-length portraits on
the walls. At one end LANGLEY has set up a table behind
which he and FENNEL sit. FENNEL is almost forty, fat,

boyish, an enthusiast, an intellectual enjoying his war.
Scattered round the room are a mixture of PLAINCLOTHES
PEOPLE, ENGINEERS and OFFICERS from the three Services.
Next to ANNA on a sofa is KARL, heavy, dark-jowelled,
bewildered. He seems to understand nothing of what is
going on.

FENNEL: This is a research unit within the Political
    Warfare Executive. How the rest of that department
    functions is none of your concern. I am your only
    contact with the world outside and I don't expect
    to visit you very often. I'm afraid you will know
    very little about the success or failure of your work.
    You are throwing stones into a pond which is a very
    long way away. And there will be almost no ripples.
    So your job must be to keep your heads down and just
    . . . keep at it, even though you'll have almost no
    idea of the effect you're having.
    (KARL leans across the sofa and whispers to ANNA.)
KARL: Ich verstehe nicht.
ANNA: *(Whispers)* Moment.
FENNEL: Perhaps even when the war is over you will not know
    what good you did.
    (FENNEL smiles.)

16. INT. DRAWING ROOM. DAY
ANNA leans alone against a window frame. Everyone is now
standing in cocktail positions. Two MAIDS pass between
groups of people pouring out beer from big, stoppered two-
pint bottles. In one group stand FENNEL, LANGLEY, ALLARDYCE.
FENNEL: I suppose you'd been hoping to represent your
    country.
LANGLEY: That's right. I was aiming for the 1940 Olympics.

(He smiles.)

FENNEL: But you still have your blue . . .

LANGLEY: Half-blue.

FENNEL: Fencing is a half-blue?

LANGLEY: That's right. But I'm still hoping for national
honour. I mean, after the war.

*(They smile. ARCHIE is sitting alone on the sofa
staring across the room at ANNA. ANNA raises the pint
mug to her lips but takes as little as possible. She
is very self-conscious and lonely. The FENNEL
conversation has moved on.)*

FENNEL: The boys on *The Times* actually got hold of an onion.

LANGLEY: Good Lord.

FENNEL: Can you imagine? Someone actually gave them one.
A whole onion. Great big thing. So they auctioned it
among the staff. Went to the night editor for £4 3s 4d.

ALLARDYCE: Well.

LANGLEY: Worth it.

(Now FENNEL seems to catch ANNA's eye. She looks away.)

FENNEL: Certainly. Of course.

*(A gong sounds. The room goes silent, caught for a
moment as they stand.)*

17.INT. DINING ROOM. DAY

*The Unit sit round a large dinner table, overhung with
chandeliers. The OLDER MAID dollops mashed potato onto
each plate as the YOUNG MAID passes with an ashet on which
sits a piece of pork luncheon meat in the shape of a tin.
She puts it down at the head of the table, and as the top
seat is unoccupied ARCHIE rises and gravely begins to
carve the luncheon meat. It makes a succulent, unpleasant
noise. ANNA looks out of the window to the drive where*

19

LANGLEY *is talking animatedly to* FENNEL *and a* NAVAL
COMMANDER. *You can just hear them speaking.*

FENNEL: Goodbye. Good luck. I'll try and get down in a
couple of months.

*(FENNEL and the COMMANDER climb into the car, gathering
up piles of paper from off the back seat. They look
to ANNA romantic and attractive. FENNEL's DRIVER
drives them away.*

*An uneasy silence as the Unit eat. KARL leans to ANNA
and whispers in German. Apologetically, ANNA speaks.)*

ANNA: He would like to know . . . what exactly we're all
doing here.

(ARCHIE looks up from his food.)

ARCHIE: Tell him he's a wireless station. Like the BBC.

18. INT. GUN ROOM. DAY

ARCHIE at the window. EILEEN with her dictation pad.
*ANNA and KARL sitting useless at the other side of the
room.*

EILEEN: The question of Hess.

ARCHIE: The question of Hess. *(He taps his knuckles on the
windowpane in a gesture of frustration.)*

ANNA: Perhaps if you told us more about it we would be able
to help.

*(EILEEN smiles. ANNA watches as ARCHIE turns and stares
at her.)*

ARCHIE: The game is. We are a radio station . . .

ANNA: Yes.

ARCHIE: Broadcasting to Germany. My job is to script the
broadcasts. Your job is to interpret them.

ANNA: I see.

KARL: Was sagt er?

20

ANNA: *(In German)* Propaganda.

ARCHIE: Yes.

(Pause.)

ARCHIE: We are to pretend to be two German army officers
stationed a thousand miles apart sending coded messages
to each other nightly over short wave radio. When the
messages have been sent, the idea is that one of our
officers - 'Otto' - will relax, he will talk more
frankly, he will add his own personal comments on the
conduct of the war. And those comments will not be
complimentary to the Nazi leaders.

ANNA: I see.

ARCHIE: Does that make sense to you?

ANNA: Of course. But it does seem a little elaborate.

(A moment. ARCHIE looks beadily at ANNA.)

ARCHIE: You fight a war, you expect propaganda, you expect
your enemy to tell you lies. Right? *(He moves across
the room towards them.)* So people spend a good deal
of their time on their guard. Now the beauty of this
idea is that when we make our first broadcast tonight,
maybe ten or fifteen people, radio hams mostly, will
twiddle their dials and stumble on it. But because
they have found us by accident, and because they appear
to be eavesdropping on a purely private conversation,
and that conversation is indubitably between loyal
army officers on their own side . . . they will be
inclined to trust everything we say. And from that
trust our influence will grow.

(ANNA looks at ARCHIE, then nods at KARL.)

ANNA: Is he one of the officers?

(ARCHIE nods.)

Who is he really?

ARCHIE: He's a Jew.   From Frankfurt.

ANNA: Shall I tell him?

    (ARCHIE nods.   ANNA turns to KARL. As ARCHIE speaks
    ANNA translates.)

ARCHIE: He will be playing the part of Otto, a loyal
    Prussian officer, broadcasting to an old friend in
    another part of Germany . . .

ANNA: *(Translating consecutively.)*
    Sie sollen die Rolle von Otto spielen, einem treuen
    preussischen Offizier, der mit einem altern Kameraden
    in einem anderen Teil Deutschlands ein Rundfunkgespräch
    führt.

KARL: Sie meinen, ich soll Theater spielen?

ANNA: Ja.

ARCHIE: The character of the Prussian must be authentic . .

ANNA: Er muss authentisch sein.

    (ARCHIE is staring at ANNA who has lost her nervousness
    for the first time.)

ARCHIE: His language will therefore be rough . . .

ANNA: Er spricht sehr roh.

ARCHIE: Corrosive . . .

ANNA: Abrupt.

ARCHIE: Obscene.

    (ANNA does not look up.   A pause.)

ANNA: Obszön.

    (KARL looks up.)

19. INT. BILLIARD ROOM.   NIGHT

The room has been converted into a wireless station, but
signs of its original function remain.   Racks of cues
stand on the walls, and there is a prominent scoreboard.
A green leather top has been laid over the baize.

Microphones have been placed at either end of the table, beside green light bulbs which flash to cue the broadcaster. At one end is KARL, at the other HERR JUNGKE. He is a small, rather effete old man with pursed lips. In the middle, like a tennis umpire, sits ALLARDYCE controlling the equipment.

Along the side of the room sit the rest of the Unit watching: ARCHIE, ANNA, EILEEN, LANGLEY.

ALLARDYCE: Stand by, please.

(A red light comes on and ALLARDYCE nods at KARL who is looking more than usually nervous and distraught.)

ALLARDYCE: You have the air.

(LANGLEY makes a sign at KARL to sit forward. The green light comes on silently in front of him.)

KARL: Hier Otto-Abend Eins . . . Hier Otto-Abend Eins.

(KARL's light goes out. He sits back. At the other end of the table JUNGKE's light comes on. He now cups one hand over his ear instinctively in response to KARL.)

JUNGKE: Ja . . . Otto . . . ich empfange . . . hast du 'ne Meldung?

(A moment, then his light goes out. He sits back with an expression of relief. At the other end KARL becomes more apprehensive then ever. His light is on. ALLARDYCE beckons at him.)

KARL: Jawohl die Meldung lautet. Mitzi muss ihren Vater treffen. Mitzi muss ihren Vater treffen.

(KARL's light goes out. JUNGKE's light comes on. We see down the whole length of the billiard table, two ludicrous figures pretending to be miles apart.)

JUNGKE: Verstanden. Na, Otto, was hältst du denn von der Flucht von Hess?

(The light bulbs change. KARL flinches.)
KARL: Ach ja, die Sache mit Hess. Tja, also . . .
   (He seems to have lost his place. ARCHIE puts his
   head in his hands. ANNA looks away.) Niemand glaubt,
   Hess sei auf Befehl des Führers nach England geflogen.
   Nein nein, er ist aus einem ganz anderen Grund nach
   England geflogen. *(ARCHIE gets up from his seat.)*
   Der Grund ist - er ist ein grosser Verbrecher, ein
   Wahnsinniger.

20. INT. TRANSMISSION ROOM. NIGHT

A disc-cutting machine is the next room. Over it sits an
ENGINEER wiping the floss from the disc as it cuts. Behind
him stands LOTTERBY.

KARL: *(V.O.)* Der Erschrekende an Hess ist nicht was er
   gemacht hat, sondern die Tatsache dass er so leicht
   ein Vertrauter Hitlers werden konnte. Als treue
   Deutsche müssen wir uns damit abfinden, dass Adolf
   Hitler bereit ist, Idioten um sich zu dulden . . .

21. EXT. HOUSE. NIGHT

The house from outside sitting confidently in the English
countryside. The moon beyond. Distorted across the
airwaves comes the continuous sound of KARL, now ranting
falteringly but with increasing vehemence. Some rabbits
pass across the lawn.

KARL: *(V.O.)* . . . Archlecker, Verbrecher, Verräter,
   solche die an Grössenwahn leiden, oder die ihre
   eigenen Mütter vergewaltigen wollen.

22. INT. BILLIARD ROOM. NIGHT

JUNGKE waves at KARL. KARL waves back.

24

JUNGKE: Auf wiedersehen.

>*(His light goes out. ALLARDYCE turns to KARL.)*

KARL: Auf wiedersehen. *(His light goes out. He sits back.*
>*ARCHIE walks straight out of the room. Silence. KARL*
>*spreads his palms on the table.)* Am sorry.

>*(LANGLEY acknowledges this with a nod. KARL speaks*
>*with terrible seriousness and difficulty.)*

>Will be good.

LANGLEY: Yes.

KARL: All Jews . . . good at showbiz.

LANGLEY: Yes. *(He gets up and smiles.)* All right everyone.

23. INT. HALL. NIGHT

The Unit comes quietly into the hall and disperses upstairs,
ANNA and EILEEN walking up together. LANGLEY crosses with
JUNGKE to the front door where LOTTERBY is waiting with
JUNGKE's coat.

LOTTERBY: Take Herr Jungke back, sir.

LANGLEY: Thank you.

>*(JUNGKE confides in LANGLEY as he puts his coat on.)*

JUNGKE: The boy is nervous.

LANGLEY: Yes.

JUNGKE: But also the script is not good. The writing . . .
>*(Rubs his fingers together.)* . . . not savage enough.

>*(A pause. LANGLEY remains expressionless.)*

LANGLEY: We'll try again tomorrow. Thank you for coming .
>. . goodnight. *(He reaches for the unseen light switch*
>*by the door and we are plunged into darkness.)*

24. EXT. SKY. NIGHT

Clouds move quickly across the moon.

25. INT. BEDROOM. NIGHT

As before but this time ANNA is asleep. Then suddenly the
door crashes open and ARCHIE bursts into the room carrying
a bottle of scotch.

ARCHIE: I'll smash a bloody bottle in yer if yer bloody
      come near me. *(He slips and falls at once to the*
      floor. The bottle smashes. Silence.)

26. INT. CORRIDOR. NIGHT

In the moonlight ANNA's door opens and she appears dragging
ARCHIE's body out into the upstairs corridor. Then when
she's got him out she turns him to point the way the corridor
goes. He does not wake. Then she goes back in. A moment
later she comes out with a blanket which she lays over him.
She goes back into her room, closes the door.

27. INT. BEDROOM. DAY

Morning light at the window. ANNA gets out of bed. Avoids
the broken glass on the floor. Takes away the chair she
has jammed under the doorhandle. She involuntarily puts
one arm over her chest as she opens the door. The corridor
is deserted. Even the blanket has gone.

28. INT. DINING ROOM. DAY

ARCHIE sits alone at the far end of the table with a bottle
of milk and a plain glass. ANNA goes over to the sideboard.
On the hotplate there is a kettle, a pan and a tin. She
opens it. Powdered eggs. She attempts normality.

ANNA: Can I make you some egg?

ARCHIE: I've had yer tea, I'd want inoculation before I
      tried yer egg . . . .

ANNA: Look, I'm quite prepared not to mention the fact . . .

26

ARCHIE: *(Shouts)* What?

> *(ANNA looks at him and walks out of the room.)*

29. INT. HALL. DAY

ANNA comes out into the deserted hall. At the bottom of the staircase a teleprinter machine is clattering out information. Then a voice comes from a distant wireless.

VOICE: This is the first news bulletin of the day and Joseph McLeod reading it. The retreat of the defeated Italian army goes on. General Wavell's message to his troops . . .

> *(ANNA stands alone in the middle of the hall.)*

ANNA: Somebody talk to me.

30. MONTAGE SEQUENCE ONE

At once we hear Chopin Waltz No 3 in A Minor. A piano segment, no more than thirty seconds. Under it we see the following images:

ARCHIE standing watching the rain coming down outside the window;

ALLARDYCE looking regretfully away as KARL blunders through another broadcast;

ANNA and EILEEN laughing together as EILEEN elaborately shows ANNA how to make a cup of tea;

LANGLEY and ALLARDYCE playing croquet on the lawn as EILEEN and ANNA sit watching. LOTTERBY stands behind them and commentates. Long cool drinks are being sipped;

ANNA before she goes to bed putting the chair against her door;

Fade. The Chopin ends.

31. INT. PASSAGE. DAY

*Outside the gun room. Most of the sporting gear has
been moved into the passage from which no one has had time
to move it. It is oddly piled alongside overspill from
inside the office. There is a pair of skis by the door.
Nailed onto the door is a trophy, a Nazi notice board;
JUDEN BETRETTEN DIESEN ORT AUF EIGENE GEFAHR. The sound
of EILEEN's typewriter as ANNA walks quickly down the
passage and into the gun room.*

32. INT. GUN ROOM. DAY

EILEEN at work on a huge pile of notes. ANNA comes in.

ANNA: Langley wants us. There's a morning conference.

EILEEN: I've still got all this stuff to do.

ANNA: They're going into Russia.

EILEEN: Who?

ANNA: The Germans.

EILEEN: Into Russia. What for?

ANNA: To make us work even harder, I suppose.

> *(EILEEN smiles.)*

33. INT. LANGLEY'S OFFICE. DAY

*A room in the front of the house. Once a gentleman's
study and library, now serving as LANGLEY's office, it has
a large open fireplace and cleared desks. It's clean,
manly and well ordered. Flowers in vases. LANGLEY sits
behind his desk opposite ARCHIE. At one side EILEEN
sits taking dictation, on the other side sits ANNA.
LANGLEY is at his most severe.*

LANGLEY: This discussion to be noted, minuted, dated 10th
> June 1941. *(EILEEN's shorthand follows.)* We have it
> from the War Cabinet that Hitler is invading Russia
> within the next two weeks. I needn't stress how

important this news is to our work. It's a military
step of extraordinary foolishness, Hitler himself
counsels against it in *Mein Kampf,* and it gives us
exactly the opportunity we've been looking for to cast
doubt on Germany's war leadership. Our loyal German
officer therefore is now in a position to condemn the
step as national suicide. He can then go on to question
the whole direction of the war.
   (Pause)
ARCHIE: May I ask a question, Will?
LANGLEY: Of course.
ARCHIE: Surely if there's a possibility of national suicide,
   that's something we'd be wanting to encourage, no? *(He
   smiles.)*
LANGLEY: I'm sorry, I don't see your point.
ARCHIE: You see I can't help looking at it another way.
   Your idea is nice, Will, I mean it's simple anyway, but
   surely one of the things we've learnt . . . attack the
   leadership direct and it always sound like propaganda.
   And anything that sounds like propaganda is not good
   propaganda.
LANGLEY: Go on.
ARCHIE: I'd say if they're going to do something foolish,
   we should encourage them. I mean let's have Otto right
   behind the idea.
LANGLEY: But you can't justify it Archie, Otto's a military
   man . . .
ARCHIE: Look, Otto says . . .
LANGLEY: He'd know that going into Russia is insane. I mean
   a war on two fronts . . .
ARCHIE: Look Otto says . . . Otto says the real enemy of
   Germany has always been Bolshevism. And now the army

is getting a chance to begin its real fight. But. It
is hard to fight Bolshevism abroad, when there are
known Bolsheviks inside the Nazi Party. So. The loyal
German is happy to die in Russia, but he is not happy
if there is any evidence of subversion at home. And
anybody . . . anybody at all who for whatever reason
dares to oppose the Russian venture, or fails to suppor
it with every sinew of their body is by definition
. . a Bolshevik. *(He smiles.)* Do y' see everybody?
Red-baiting! *(He laughs and claps his hands together.)*
Anyone who speaks out is branded as a Bolshevik.
Criticism silenced. Millions die. *(Pause. LANGLEY
stares at him.)* Well? Is that no' what ye want?

34. INT. GUN ROOM. NIGHT

*Blacked out windows. A single green light. EILEEN has a
single sheet of paper in her hand, which she reads out.
ARCHIE is sitting on the desk. LANGLEY, ANNA are watching.
KARL is tucked away, his lips moving slightly as EILEEN
reads. There is a new concentration in the work. EILEEN
reads well.*

EILEEN: Many will die. Many will be happy to die on the
road to Moscow as long as they feel they have the
efforts of the whole nation concentrated behind them.
For those who stay at home have a duty too. They have
a duty to keep morale high, to silence dissent.
*(ARCHIE nods at LANGLEY to signal approval of the
idea.)*
There will not be enough food this winter, there will
not be enough clothes. Everyone must therefore try
to discover those Party members who are taking more
than their rations. Everyone will have to be vigilant,

everyone will have to be a spy. It is a great
adventure. We must all be ruthless in its pursuit.
Goodnight my friend. My dear, dear friend. *(She
looks up. They look at her, awed.)*

35. INT. BILLIARD ROOM. NIGHT
*The red light goes on. KARL bends forward. He is
transformed. We follow his delivery - iron, witty,
inflected. Sweat pours from him. His voice is much
deeper then before.*

KARL: Viele werden sterben. Viele werden froh sein auf
dem Wege nach Moskau zu sterben, solange sie wissen,
dass das ganze Volk ihnen beisteht. *(We look at the
Unit sitting at the side, as if deeply moved by what
he is saying.)* Aber die, die zu Hause bleiben, haben
auch eine Aufgabe. Ihre Aufgabe ist es, die Moral
des Volkes zu heben und Gegner zum Schweigen zu
bringen. Es wird in diesem Winter nicht genug zu
essen geben, nicht genug Kleidung. *(ARCHIE smiles.
We go back to KARL.)* Jeder muss also versuchen
herauszufinden, welche Parteimiglieder mehr als
ihre Rationen bekommen. Jeder muss wachsam sein.
Jeder muss Spion sein. Es ist ein grosses Abenteuer.
Wir müssen rücksichtslos sein. Gute Nacht lieber
Freund, mein lieber, lieber Freund. *(The red light
goes off and KARL takes off his glasses. LANGLEY
smiles.)*

LANGLEY: Superb!

36. INT. HALL. NIGHT
*At once Chopin again. Odd, lilting, deft. LANGLEY and
ARCHIE seen from behind going down corridor together.*

31

ARCHIE: We've hit a vein.

LANGLEY: We have. More again tomorrow?

ARCHIE: Certainly.

LANGLEY: This Russian business . . . could be the making
     of us.

     *(As they turn into the drawing room ARCHIE uncharacter-
     istically performs a tiny dance step.)*

37. INT. DRAWING ROOM. NIGHT

*JUNGKE sits playing Chopin. His face is angelic, his feet
barely touch the pedals. The Steinway has been pulled
out from the wall, and the Unit have flopped down round
the room. EILEEN is reading 'Wellington Wendy', LANGLEY
is reading 'The Times'. The ENGINEERS are playing chess.
ANNA sits staring on a sofa as behind her ARCHIE moves
very slowly, decanter in hand. He stops immediately behind
her, pours out a glass very steadily and moves on. She does
not turn. JUNGKE leans in to perform an intricate arpeggio.
Then LOTTERBY appears at the door with JUNGKE's coat.*

LOTTERBY: The car for Herr Jungke, sir.

     *(JUNGKE stops playing. LANGLEY gets up from his seat,
     speaks slowly to him.)*

LANGLEY: We have something for you.

     *(LOTTERBY crosses to the piano and helps JUNGKE up as
     LANGLEY goes to the sideboard where a bottle sits on
     a tray with a little dish beside it. LOTTERBY brings
     JUNGKE back and sits him in LANGLEY's empty chair.
     LANGLEY ceremoniously carries the tray and sets it
     down beside JUNGKE.)*

LANGLEY: Sambuca.

JUNGKE: Do you have . . . a coffee bean?

     (LANGLEY takes the dish and puts one coffee bean in

32

the liquid then takes out a box of matches and sets
light to it. *JUNGKE looks at the flame.)*

JUNGKE: It is payment enough. Thank you.

(LANGLEY looks up at LOTTERBY.)

LANGLEY: Ian, would you take Herr Jungke back to the
internment camp?

LOTTERBY: Sir.

38. INT. HALL. NIGHT

*JUNGKE is being escorted out by LANGLEY. LOTTERBY waits
for them.*

JUNGKE: It's not too bad. I have to be in solitary because
of this work but there are compensations. I have
books, you know. And I had a letter once.
*(ANNA and EILEEN cross the hall and go upstairs on
their way to bed.)*

EILEEN: Archie's drunk again.

ANNA: Why does he drink so much?

EILEEN: I don't know. Fleet Street, I suppose. They all
do.

ANNA: Was he a journalist?

39. INT. STAIRS. NIGHT

ANNA and EILEEN on the servants' stairs.

EILEEN: By the time the war came he was on one of the big
national dailies. Fought his way up.

ANNA: From?

EILEEN: Poverty. Terrible. He comes from Glasgow, from
the Red Clyde. You must know that.

ANNA: I don't know anything.

40. INT. BEDROOM. NIGHT

ANNA comes into her bedroom. Closes the door. She then picks up the chair to put it under the handle. But then pauses with the chair in her hand. Turns. Puts the chair back where it came from. Goes instead into the bathroom.

41. INT. BEDROOM. NIGHT
As before. ANNA's face, asleep. We are very close.
ARCHIE: *(V.O.)* Woman.
> *(A moment, then ANNA opens her eyes. She does not move. The sound of ripping material.)*
> *(V.O.)* I'm at yer feet.
> *(ANNA scrambles up the bed and stands on top of it. By this time she can make out the figure of ARCHIE at the bottom of the bed. He is very serious and very drunk.)*
> The Scotsman's approach to the art a' love-makin'.
> *(Pause)* The Scot makes love wi' a broken bottle.
> An' a great deal a' screamin'. *(Pause)* There'll be
> a moment while I take off ma clothes. *(He disappears beneath the end of the bed. There is a pause. ANNA peers forward, into the dark.)*

42. INT. BEDROOM. NIGHT
ANNA lying in bed with the sheet pulled up around her. She is soaked in sweat, her hair in strands. There is a light on in the bathroom and the door is ajar. You can see a trousered leg and hear the sound of water in a bowl. ANNA barely turns towards the figure.
ANNA: I literally didn't know there was such a thing as an electricity bill. I was sheltered, I suppose. Where we live we just always left the lights on. I assumed the electricity just came . . . it just came and you

paid your taxes and you got your light. Then the
other day I was talking to Eileen and she said
electricity prices had risen, and I said, you mean you
have to pay? For what you use? You have to pay? Gas,
electricity, water. It had never occurred to me.
(Silence. She shivers.) Archie. I am trying to learn.
*(The light goes out in the bathroom. ARCHIE walks
silently through the bedroom, opens the door and goes
out. ANNA alone.)*

43. INT. KITCHEN. DAY

*Daylight flooding in at the kitchen window. ANNA is sitting
on the table with her back to us as EILEEN carefully steams
open envelopes over a boiling kettle. She then sorts the
letters out into two piles.*

EILEEN: *(Sorting through letters.)* German . . . German for
    you . . . English for me . . . German . . . English.
    (ANNA casually picks one up.)

ANNA: Who wrote them?

EILEEN: Just ordinary people in Germany writing to their
    relatives in the States.

ANNA: I didn't know they were allowed to.

EILEEN: Why not? America's neutral.

ANNA: Then how did we get hold of them?

EILEEN: Not that neutral, apparently. English . . .

ANNA: What are we meant to do with them?

EILEEN: You'll have to ask Genius.

ANNA: Is he down?

EILEEN: In the office.

ANNA: Ah.

    (ANNA goes. EILEEN continues to read her letters.)

EILEEN: Whoops. Somebody's dead.

44. INT. GUN ROOM. DAY

ARCHIE at his desk writing flowingly with a fountain pen.
Bright morning light behind him. Around him fresh supplies
of office stationery, including two piles of files almost
ceiling-high. On one wall is pinned a new map of Germany.
He doesn't look up as ANNA comes in. She stands at the
door with a fistful of letters.

ANNA: I want to know what to do with these.

(ARCHIE looks at her, referring to the piles of
stationery.)

ARCHIE: I shall be opening files on named individuals.
While their army is in Russia we shall be looking for
examples of favouritism at home. How Nazi Party
officials get more food, get more clothes, than
ordinary people. How they get sugar. How they get
fruit. How they get wine. How they give parties in
private rooms where cakes full of raisins and marzipan
are eaten. Outrageous things. You have to comb through
these letters, and open files on any named official,
you have to pick out from the gossip any hard fact, any
details of their way of life, any indiscretion, any
sign that they're enjoying themselves more than their
brothers-in-arms. This way we drive a wedge between
the Party and the people. We broadcast real names,
plausible offences, backed up with thorough research.

(He looks at ANNA, then returns to writing.)

ANNA: And when we've finished with the letters . . . ?

ARCHIE: Yes.

ANNA: Do we send them on?

(ARCHIE stares at her.)

ARCHIE: Yes. We send them on.

(ARCHIE returns to writing. ANNA moves across the room

> sharply and puts the letters down on his desk.)

ANNA: Mr Maclean.

ARCHIE: Yes. *(This time he does not look up at ANNA.)*

ANNA; I have to go to the medicine cupboard.

ARCHIE: Yes.

ANNA: I have some bruises.

ARCHIE: Yes.

> *(Nothing. ANNA turns to go.)*

45. INT. LANGLEY'S OFFICE. DAY

FENNEL in a big chair with a pot of coffee. He looks more crumpled and effusive than ever. He talks in a fast stream which LANGLEY can barely intercept.

FENNEL: We now have four stations like yours, Will, each
pretending to be an individual broadcasting from within
Germany. Of course none of this would be necessary if
we could persuade the BBC to take a less literal
attitude to what they like to call the truth, but I'm
afraid that they do go on insisting that when the
Navy says it's sunk a sub, it does actually have to
have sunk a sub. So I can't see us getting much joy
out of them. So what I'd like to do is co-ordinate
all intelligence outlets, and start a Rumour Committee
which will take charge of all misleading information,
so we don't find ourselves with lots of little rumours
popping up all over the place, but put all our efforts
into good big sharp vicious rumours that really do the
job . . . .

> *(A knock at the door.)*

LANGLEY: Come in.

> *(ANNA enters.)*

ANNA: I'm sorry, I just want the medicine chest.

37

LANGLEY: Yes, of course. Come in.

(LANGLEY goes to get it down from a high cabinet.
FENNEL goes on, ignoring ANNA.)

FENNEL: It'll be a high-level Committee; Sandy, Gargs,
Freddy if we have to, God help us, weekly meetings,
decide who to go for . . .

LANGLEY: Yes.

FENNEL: Mostly the smaller fish, but go hard . . .

LANGLEY: Yes.

FENNEL: It's the little chap, the local leader we can really
destroy, smears, innuendo, well co-ordinated . . .

LANGLEY: Yes.

FENNEL: Anyway we'll send you Rumour Directives, they'll
come on G2s of course, when you get the G2 for Christ's
sake don't forget to cross-file . . . .

(LANGLEY hands a white box with a red cross to ANNA.)

LANGLEY: Here you are.

ANNA: Thank you.

FENNEL: I hope you're settling down all right, my dear.
Don't find it all too high-powered.

(ANNA smiles, not knowing what to say. She clutches
the box.)

Your uncle was very angry with me. Said I'd sent you
to work for a savage.

(ANNA looks at LANGLEY.)

LANGLEY: I think he means Maclean.

ANNA: I see.

FENNEL: That's right.

(ANNA opens the medicine box and searches through it.
They look at her as if expecting her to say more.)

The Celtic race, you know: a cloven-hoofed people.
They do seem to be fighting quite a different war.

ANNA: He seems . . . he just seems a very extraordinary
      man to me. *(She turns and looks at them defiantly.*
      Then refers to a bottle.) Is this Dettol?
LANGLEY: That's what it says.

46. INT. BEDROOM. DAY
ANNA sitting on the edge of her bed. She lifts her skirt
up and undoes a suspender. Pulls down her stocking. On
her upper thigh, scratch and bruise marks. She applies the
Dettol with cotton wool. Tears come into her eyes. She
works down her thigh. Tears flow now, silently. Without
sobbing, she just lets the tears run down her cheek.

47. MONTAGE SEQUENCE TWO
Chopin again. The same segment. Under it we see:
EILEEN hard at work at night, typing furiously;
KARL broadcasting, a look of extreme vindictiveness
colouring his face;
The Unit sitting round a dinner table heavy with Christmas
decoration. ANNA comes into the dining room with a soufflé
she has obviously just cooked. Everyone applauds;
ANNA getting out of bed in the morning. She removes an
empty whisky bottle from the bedside table and takes it to
the wardrobe. There she sets it in a rank next to six
other empty bottles which are stacked on a high shelf
next to her teddy;
Fade. Chopin ends.

48. INT. PASSAGE. Day
Now almost impassable. A line of filing cabinets is banked
along one wall. Opposite several thousand loose files and
complete editions of German and English newspapers. LANGLEY

comes down with a file and finds ANNA sitting on the floor
in the corridor doing her work. She is wrapped in many
sweaters against the cold. He refers into the gun room.

LANGLEY: What's happening?

ANNA: One of his moods. What's that?

LANGLEY: German prisoners of war. Interrogated by
    Intelligence. Very gratifying. Look. (He opens the
    file and hands it to ANNA. From inside the room you
    can hear EILEEN's typewriter and ARCHIE's odd bad-
    tempered grunt.) They report a run on clothing in
    Berlin. It's impossible to buy an overcoat because
    of rumours that Nazi party official are soon to get
    special clothing privileges.

ANNA: Amazing.

LANGLEY: They're issuing denials but to no effect. All
    our own work. It's proof someone's listening. I'll
    show it to him.

ANNA: He wouldn't want to know. It would spoil the game.
    (They smile.)

ARCHIE: (V.O. rudely.) Anna.

49. INT. GUN ROOM. DAY

The room is now a fat stew of paperwork. Towers of documents
take up most of the room. ARCHIE is strained and tired.
EILEEN, who like ANNA is well wrapped, is barely keeping her
patience with him. ANNA comes in.

ARCHIE: I have chosen Cologne. I have chosen the Burgomaster
    in Cologne. Now what do we have?
    (ANNA looks round the room confused.)

ANNA: Eileen, is Cologne in the lavatory?

EILEEN: No, no it's over there somewhere.
    (ANNA heads where EILEEN pointed, flicks through.)

ARCHIE: Eileen. Prisoner interrogation. Anything we have

from the cages to do with Cologne.

(EILEEN gets up and goes out.)

50. INT. PASSAGE. DAY

LANGLEY is standing listening outside the door, unseen by
ARCHIE. As EILEEN comes out to get a file, she turns
back towards the room and mimes machine-gunning ARCHIE
to death. LANGLEY smiles and squeezes her arm. EILEEN
just nods and sets to work. LANGLEY heads off down the
corridor, casually tossing the file he had brought onto
a random pile.

51. INT. GUN ROOM. DAY

ANNA lays out what she's collected on ARCHIE's desk, taking
it all from one fat file.

ANNA: Street directory. Train timetable. Party structure.

ARCHIE: Ah. *(He takes that out and studies it.)*

ANNA: Bus timetables. Guide to the museum. Plan of the

sewers, any use? *(She smiles, he takes no notice.)*

ARCHIE: His name is Duffendorf. Lutz Duffendorf, Burgomaster

of Cologne, please. *(This last to ANNA who goes to a*
wall cabinet for a file card system. EILEEN meanwhile
is back from the corridor.)

EILEEN: Cologne's pretty good. Eighteen separate

interrogations, three or four look good.

ANNA: *(To herself.)* D - Duffendorf.

ARCHIE: I need a woman, Eileen. Find me a woman of

doubtful reputation.

EILEEN: I'll see. *(As she goes to search, ANNA returns,*
with a white card.)

ANNA: Lutz Duffendorf. Age forty-three. Bookseller's son.

41

Married. No children.

ARCHIE: No children.

ANNA: His wife is blind.

ARCHIE: Wife blind. How wonderful.

ANNA: There's a picture. *(She detaches a newspaper photo
    from the card and shows it to ARCHIE holding a pencil
    over the man's face. An official dinner at which
    a group of Germans are conspicuously well-fed.
    Duffendorf is fat and slack. ARCHIE stares at him.
    Meanwhile, EILEEN has found a suitable detail.)*

EILEEN: Someone in the parachute regiment mentions a green-
    grocer, and his wife, in Blumenstrasse. She sounds
    what you're looking for.

ARCHIE: Good. *(He reaches down behind his desk and gets
    out three large volumes.)* Kraft-Ebbing. Havelock
    Ellis. And Kleinwort's *Dictionary of Sexual Perversion*.
    Start at the index, right? *(He hands the dictionary
    to ANNA. EILEEN is about to protest.)*

EILEEN: Is this . . . *(But ARCHIE just looks at her and
    she turns away. ANNA opens the book, then begins
    reading dispassionately.)*

ANNA: Fantasies?

ARCHIE: Yes.

ANNA: Male fantasies. Judge. Air pilot. Hanged man. Horse.
    Snake charmer. Roman Catholic Priest . . . .

ARCHIE: All right. Off fantasies.

ANNA: Fetishes?

ARCHIE: Yes.

ANNA: Food. Rope. Rubber. Leather . . . .

ARCHIE: Look up leather. *(ANNA looks at ARCHIE, but he cuts
    her off before she speaks.)* It will do. Eileen.
    (EILEEN waits, pad in hand, patiently. ANNA looks up

the reference.) You won't believe this, old friend, what . . .

EILEEN: Duffendorf.

ARCHIE: . . . what Duffendorf's been up to. Everyone in Cologne is talking about what the telegram boy saw when he looked through the letterbox trying to deliver. What he saw was the Burgomaster trying to deliver the Frau . . .

ANNA: *(Not looking up.)* That pun won't translate.

EILEEN: Ilse Schmidt.

ARCHIE: Trying to deliver to Frau Ilse Schmidt. Well we know how many people have been down that particular path before. But what is unusual is what she was wearing . . . *(ARCHIE holds out his hand. ANNA heaves across the open book.)* A leather bathing costume. *(EILEEN is about to protest, when ARCHIE jabs viciously at the book with his finger.)* It says here. *(ANNA smiles.)* A leather bathing costume. And him standing with a hosepipe in his hand. *(A pause. He closes his eyes.)* Well, well, you ask why does she consent? It doesn't sound like pleasure in the ordinary sense of the word. It is not. It is corruption. In return for her performance the Burgomaster is using his influence to secure her a supply of fresh fruit and vegetables which she will sell at inflated prices. While our countrymen are dying on the Russian front, she will exploit their families at home. And meanwhile even as they romp, above the obscene display there sits an old woman locked in her room. The Burgomaster's wife. *(His coup de grâce.)* Alone. Listening. And blind.

52. INT. EILEEN'S ROOM. NIGHT

An identical room to ANNA's but EILEEN has made it more
homely with photographs and a dressing table stacked with
make-up. EILEEN is sitting at it in her slip, getting
ready for dinner. ANNA stands behind her, already
dressed. They are laughing.

EILEEN: He is going mad.

ANNA: D' you think so?

EILEEN: I'm sure. He is barking mad. *(They both laugh.*
EILEEN looks at herself in the mirror intently. Then
at ANNA pacing behind her.) Are you having a thing
with him?

ANNA: I suppose so. I suppose that's what a thing is.
(A pause. EILEEN smiles.)

EILEEN: What does he really think about . . ?

ANNA: I don't know. I don't know what he thinks about
anything. We've never had a conversation. We just
have a thing. *(She looks down at EILEEN. Then bursts*
out laughing.) Isn't life wonderful?

53. INT. HALL. NIGHT

The Unit going in to dinner. ANNA and EILEEN come down
the stairs together. LANGLEY is standing outside his
office as they come down. He moves across to intercept
them.

LANGLEY: Eileen. There's somebody to see you.

EILEEN: Oh, really?

LANGLEY: Would you like to use my room?

(EILEEN goes in. LANGLEY closes the door behind her
but we just glimpse a UNIFORMED OFFICER as the door
shuts. ANNA is left standing looking across at LANGLEY.)
Her brother has been killed. Singapore.

(ANNA *stands completely stunned by the news. LANGLEY*
watches. Then she speaks quietly.)
ANNA: Oh God . . . .

54. INT. EILEEN'S ROOM. NIGHT
ANNA and EILEEN in each other's arms rocking backwards and
forwards. EILEEN is hysterical with grief, wild, out of
control, like a drowning woman. The make-up has scarred
her face. She is screaming.
EILEEN: All the time . . . .
ANNA: Yes, I know . . . .
EILEEN: All the time . . . .
ANNA: I know.
EILEEN: All the time we've been here . . . .
ANNA: Yes.
EILEEN: All the time, all the time we've been here.
ANNA: Yes I know.
EILEEN: I can't stand it. I can't stand it.
ANNA: No.
EILEEN: I can't stand what we've done.

55. INT. HALL. NIGHT
In the darkness a single shaft of light falls on EILEEN's
cases stacked by the door. The OFFICER we have glimpsed
comes across and picks up her coat which is draped across
them. Then EILEEN comes into frame, still crying gently.
He puts the coat round her shoulders, picks up her handbag.
Then leans across her and whispers quietly. The tiny
scuffles of grief. ANNA watches in an upstairs doorway.

56. INT. GUN ROOM. NIGHT
ANNA enters the darkened room with a cup of tea. ARCHIE is

standing staring at the blacked-out window, his back to
the door.

ANNA: Do you want this?

ARCHIE: Just put it down.

    (ANNA crosses to the desk and puts tea on it.)

ARCHIE: What time is it?

ANNA: Two.

ARCHIE: Has she gone?

ANNA: Mmm-mm. *(Pause)* You should have said goodbye to her

ARCHIE: What?

ANNA: That was the decent thing to do.

    (ARCHIE turns and moves towards the desk.)

ARCHIE: There's a broadcast here I've just completed. I
    want it transmitted as fast as possible. You'll also
    have to take on Eileen's secretarial tasks. Get
    right down to it in the morning will you?

ANNA: No I won't.

    (Pause. ARCHIE looks at ANNA.)

ARCHIE: I set maself the task. Get through the war. Just
    get through it, that's all. Put it no higher than
    that. Accept it. Endure it. But don't think, because
    if you begin to think, it'll all come apart in your
    hands. So. Let's all have the time of our lives not
    bothering to think about a bloody thing. Just . . .
    get on with it. This house is the war. And I'd
    rather be anywhere, I'd rather be in France, I'd
    rather be in the desert, I'd rather be in a Wellington
    over Berlin, anywhere but here with you and your people
    in this bloody awful English house . . . but I shall
    spend it here.

    (Pause)

ANNA: Strange thing; as if to suffer and say nothing were

        clever. As if to do this degrading work were clever.
        As if that were clever. *(Long pause.)* Will you hold
        me? Will you touch me?
ARCHIE: No. *(He looks down.)*

57. INT. BEDROOM. NIGHT
*ANNA sits dressed on her bed reading ARCHIE's script. We
look at the pages. They are a mass of scrawled instructions
and underlinings. There are Stars of David scratched in
bright red ink, there are exclamation marks and enormous
phrases like 'Now look here', and 'Stress this'.
Some phrases refer to disease and corruption. We look at
ANNA again. She regularly puts the sheets aside. Her
face is dead.*

58. INT. LANGLEY'S OFFICE. DAY
*LANGLEY working at his desk, looks up. ANNA standing at
the door. Bright morning light.*
ANNA: There's a broadcast here. I'm not sure it's quite
        right.
LANGLEY: Come in. *(ANNA comes in and sits down opposite
        him at the desk.)* Tell me about it.
ANNA: Well . . . apparently one of Goebbels's newspapers
        has singled out for special praise the work of some
        doctors on the Russian front who run blood transfusion
        units and who've been successful in saving many,
        many lives.
LANGLEY: Yes.
ANNA: Now our idea in reply is to say that the units are
        getting their supplies of blood not from good clean
        fellow Germans, but from Polish and Russian prisoners
        who have not even had a Wassermann test. In other

words our job is to convince an army which we believe
has just sustained the most appalling losses in the
history of human warfare that those of them who have
managed to escape death are on the point of being
consumed with veneral disease.

(There is a pause. LANGLEY spreads his hands.)

LANGLEY: It sounds a very good idea.

ANNA: You don't think he's mad? You don't think, clinically,
Archie Maclean is mad?

(Pause)

LANGLEY: We don't really know what's happening on the
Russian front. But people are telling us that one
million Germans have died in Russia in the last eight
months. And of those maybe half have been killed in
battle. The rest have just curled up in their
greatcoats and died. Of frostbite. Exposure. Well
nobody in that party went of their own accord. They
went because they were inspired to go. By that great
genius Joseph Goebbels. And they stayed, in part,
because of the work he is doing. And because of that
work, they are still there. And they are still
dying. Now if you want to tell me that you can't
draft that broadcast, then you had best return to
your country estate; because we have as much duty
to assist our side as he has his. And we must bring
to it the same vigour, the same passion, the same
intelligence that he has brought to his. And if this
involves throwing a great trail of aniseed across
Europe, if it means covering the whole continent in
obloquy and filth . . . then that is what we shall do.
*(A pause. ANNA quite lost. LANGLEY looks across at
her.)* There has been a complaint about you. From

Maclean. He spoke to me this morning. Your German is
good and so is your application. But he feels from
the start you have tried to compromise him. I put it
another way. You have tried unsuccessfully to get
him to sleep with you. Please. There is the question
of legality - your age. Also Maclean knows something
of your background, your family, how little you know
of the world, and felt to take advantage would be
indefensible. And he has come to feel that the
pressure is now intolerable and rather than have to
upset you in person, he has asked me to request you to
resign.

ANNA: But it's not true.

LANGLEY: I don't care if it's true. You have unbalanced one
of our most gifted writers. That is unforgivable.
*(A pause. LANGLEY takes out a clean piece of stationery
from his desk drawer and pushes it across the desk with
a fountain pen.)* A letter of resignation.

ANNA: No.

LANGLEY: Otherwise I shall have to speak to your father,
tell him what's occurred.

ANNA: But it's not true, it's not what happened. None of
it's true.

LANGLEY: Then why did he say it?
(Silence. We look at ANNA.)

ANNA: No.

59. BLANK SCREEN.

VOICE: Five months later in July 1942, Otto Abend Eins
made his final broadcast.

60. INT. BILLIARD ROOM. NIGHT.

The Unit gathered round the table, minus ANNA, EILEEN
and ARCHIE. But FENNEL is present this time watching
from the side. KARL is in full flood. JUNGKE is
listening.

KARL: Die deutsche Wehrmacht muss härter kämpfen, muss
    den Krieg mit einer Rücksichtslosigkeit führen, die
    sie bisher nicht gezeight hat. Dieser Defaitismus
    frisst den Willen der deutschen Nation auf.
    (LANGLEY cues LOTTERBY who then bangs his rifle butt
    against the inside of the door very loudly, so loudly
    the door almost splinters. Then the door is thrown
    open from the other side and ARCHIE is revealed
    standing with a machine-gun. He runs into the room
    and jumps on top of the billiard table.)
    Um Gotteswillen!

ARCHIE: Also. Otto. Wir haben ihn gefunden. *(He points*
    the machine-gun at KARL.)

KARL: Nein, nein! Bitte! Nicht!
    (LANGLEY cues again. ARCHIE fires the machine-gun
    deafeningly loud. KARL reels back clutching himself
    and moaning. His chair goes over and he falls to the
    floor.)

ARCHIE: Also . . . *(ARCHIE strides to the wireless equipment*
    and in a huge gesture rips the cables out. Moves to
    stand over.) Otto ist tot.
    (With a creak KARL sits up from his dead position.
    His face breaks into a huge grin.)

61. EXT. HOUSE. DAY

The house seen from the outside. Its main doors are
opened and out from it come the SOLDIERS and their
SERGEANT carrying out office and wireless equipment.

*FENNEL, with his NAVAL COMMANDER, follows them and gets
into his car. LANGLEY shakes his hand.*

VOICE: The work of the department continued until the end
    of the war when all its official records were destroyed.
    Many of the most brilliant men from the Propaganda and
    Intelligence Services went on to careers in public
    life, in Parliament, Fleet Street, the universities
    and the BBC.

62. EXT. COUNCIL ESTATE. DAY

*FENNEL moves in an election van, speaking on the back of
a jeep which is plastered with photos of himself and the
slogan 'Let's Go With Labour'.*

VOICE: John Fennel resumed a career in politics which took
    him in 1968 to a Cabinet rank which he lost with
    Labour's subsequent defeat in 1970.

63. EXT. NURSING HOME. DAY

*LANGLEY in his bathchair being wheeled across a lawn by
an obviously expensive PRIVATE NURSE. He looks ill and
drawn.*

VOICE: Will Langley went on to become a world-famous
    thriller writer in the mid-fifties. His work helped
    to establish a genre notable for its sustained passages
    of sexuality and violence. He died in 1962.

64. EXT. GOLF COURSE. DAY

*Amateur film. The sound of a projector. EILEEN GRAHAM
on the golf course, looking much older, in a sensible
skirt and windcheater. She fools around for the camera.*

VOICE: Eileen Graham started a chain of employment
    agencies specializing in temporary secretaries. She

is President of the Guild of British Businesswomen.
She has never married.

65. INT. VIEWING THEATRE. NIGHT
*ARCHIE MACLEAN viewing rushes. He is sitting forward,
the beam of the projector behind his shoulder.*
VOICE: Archie Maclean was transferred that year to the
Crown Film Unit where he made distinguished
documentaries. He became known in the fifties for
his award-winning feature films . . .

66. INT. SLUM HOUSE. DAY
*A sequence from ARCHIE's black and white film, made in the
late fifties. A small boy watches as his FATHER is washed
in a tin bath by his MOTHER.*
VOICE: . . . which he both wrote and directed. The most
famous example is 'A Kind of Life', a loving and
lyrical evocation of his own childhood in Glasgow.
But his most recent work starring some of Hollywood's
best-loved names . . .

67. EXT. SEA. DAY
*A sequence from one of ARCHIE's latest films. A runaway
car speeds off the end of a pier and crashes into the water.*
VOICE: . . . has commanded little of the same critical
attention or respect.

68. BLANK SCREEN
VOICE: Anna Seaton.

69. STILLS SEQUENCE
ANNA in a sequence of black and white stills is seen in an

advertising agency leaning over an ARTIST's shoulder
to look at a drawing of a comic dog.

VOICE: Entered advertising in 1946 where she remained for
ten years, increasingly distressed at the compromises
forced on her by her profession. In 1956 she resigned
and announced her intention to live an honest life.

70. STILLS SEQUENCE

A semi-detached in Fulham, seen from outside.

VOICE: She told her husband she was having an affair with
another man, and could no longer bear the untruths of
adultery. Her husband left her.

71. STILLS SEQUENCE

A brightly lit hospital seen from outside.

VOICE: After a period of lavish promiscuity she suffered
an infected womb and an enforced hysterectomy.

72. STILLS SEQUENCE

Grosvenor Square demonstrations, 1968.

VOICE: She became a full-time researcher for the Labour
Party, until she left during the Vietnam demonstrations
and went to live with a young unmarried mother in
Wales.

73. STILLS SEQUENCE

ANNA, much older, playing on a Welsh hillside with a small
GIRL and a dog.

VOICE: Having travelled to see Maclean's latest film at a
seaside Odeon she was driven to write to him for the
first time since 1942, complaining of the falseness of
his films, the way they sentimentalized what she knew

53

to be his appalling childhood, and lamenting, in sum,
the films' lack of political direction. The last
paragraph of her letter read:

74. INT. HOUSE. DAY

*Shots of the empty rooms inside the house after the Unit
have gone. Dining room. Drawing room. Bedroom. Gun
room. All empty, standing deserted.*

ANNA: *(V.O.)* It is only now that I fully understand the
events that passed between us so many years ago. You
must allow for my ignorance, I was born into a class
and at a time that protected me from even a chance
acquaintance with the world. But since that first day
at Wendlesham I have been trying to learn, trying to
keep faith with the shame and anger I saw in you. In
retrospect what you sensed then has become blindingly
clear to the rest of us: that whereas we knew exactly
what we were fighting against, none of us had the
whisper of an idea as to what we were fighting for.
Over the years I have been watching the steady
impoverishment of the people's ideals, their loss of
faith, the lying, the daily inveterate lying, the
thirty-year-old deep corrosive national habit of lying
and I have remembered you. I have remembered the one
lie you told to make me go away. And I now at last
have come to understand why you told it. I loved you
then and I love you now. For thirty years you have
been the beat of my heart. Please, please tell me it
is the same for you.

75. EXT. HOUSE. DAY

The house seen from outside.

VOICE: He never replied.

   (The house sits in the sun. A few seconds, then:)

76. END CREDITS

Chopin's Waltz No 3 in A Minor.

A LECTURE

Given At King's College, Cambridge
March 5 1978

To begin with the obvious: the playwright writes plays.
He chooses plays as his way of speaking. If he could
speak more clearly in a lecture, he would lecture; if
polemic suited him, he'd be a journalist. But he chooses
the theatre as the most subtle and complex way of
addressing an audience he can find. Because of that, I
used to turn down all invitations to speak in public,
because I didn't want an audience to hear the tone of my
voice. I don't like the idea that they can get a hand-
down version of my plays sitting in a lecture hall and
sizing me up. In the theatre I am saying complex and
difficult things. I do not want them reduced either by my
views on the world, or, more important, the audience's idea
of my views. I want no preconceptions. I don't want,
'Oh, of course Hare is a well-known anti-vivisectionist,
that's why there's that scene where the dog is disembowelled'.
I want the dog cut up and the audience deciding for themselves if they like the sight or not. The first lesson the
playwright learns is that he is not going to be able to
control an audience's reactions anyway; if he writes an
eloquent play about the sufferings of the Jews in the Warsaw
Ghetto there is always going to be someone in the audience
who comes out completely satisfied with the evening, saying
at last someone's had the guts to say it, those Nazis knew
what they were about. As you can't control people's
reactions to your plays, your duty is also not to reduce
people's reactions, not to give them easy handles with

which they can pigeon-hole you, and come to comfortable terms with what you are saying.

So why, then, am I changing tack and beginning to try and speak a little in public about the theatre? It is partly because I have been trying in the last few months to put my ear to the ground and find out what a particular section of my audience is thinking and feeling; but it is also for other and very pressing reasons which I hope will become clear as I go on.

I'd like to start with a story which has always taken my breath away, from Hardy's incomparable novel *Jude the Obscure*. The young mother, homeless in Oxford, living in appalling poverty with a family she cannot possibly support, puts her head in her hands, and says in the presence of her eldest boy, 'O, it is better if we had never been born.' Later that day she goes upstairs. 'At the back of the door were fixed two hooks for hanging garments, and from these the forms of [her] two youngest children were suspended, by a piece of box-cord round each of their necks, while from a nail a few yards off the body of little Jude was hanging in a similar manner. An overturned chair was near the elder boy, and his glazed eyes were slanted into the room; but those of the girl and the baby boy were closed.'

I always think this is the ultimate cautionary tale for playwrights. That someone will actually take you at your word. That you will whip yourself up into a fine frenzy of dramatic writing on stage, have your superbly played heroine step harrowingly to the front of the stage and cry out in despair, 'It is better that we had never been born,' and there will in fact be an answering shot from the back of the stalls and one of the customers will slump down dead
58

having committed the sin of assuming that the playwright means what he says.

For this is an austere and demanding medium. It is a place where the playwright's ultimate sincerity and good faith is going to be tested and judged in a way that no other medium demands. As soon as a word is spoken on stage it is tested. As soon as a line is put into the reconstruction of a particular event, it will be judged. In this way the theatre is the exact opposite art to journalism; the journalist throws off a series of casual and half-baked propositions, ill-considered, dashed-off, entertainment pieces to put forward a point of view which may or may not amuse, which may or may not be lasting, which may or may not be true; but were he once to hear those same words spoken out loud in a theatre he would begin to feel that terrible chill of being collectively judged and what had seemed light and trenchant and witty would suddenly seem flip and arch and silly.

Judgement. Judgement is at the heart of the theatre. A man steps forward and informs the audience of his intention to lifelong fidelity to his wife, while his hand, even as he speaks, drifts at random to the body of another woman. The most basic dramatic situation you can imagine; the gap between what he says he is and what we see him to be opens up, and in that gap we see something that makes theatre unique; that it exposes the difference between what a man says and what he does. That is why nothing on stage is so exciting as a great lie; why *Brassneck* never recovers as a play after its greatest liar is killed off at the end of the first act.

I would suggest to you crudely that one of the reasons for the theatre's possible authority, and for its recent general drift towards politics, is its unique suitability to displaying an age in which men's ideals and men's practice bear no relation to each other; in which the public profession of, for example, socialism has often been reduced by the passage of history to wearying personal fetish, or even chronic personality disorder. The theatre is the best way of showing the gap between what is said and what is seen to be done, and that is why, ragged and gap-toothed as it is, it has still a far healthier potential than some of the other, poorer, abandoned arts.

To explain what I mean I should tell you of a conversation I once had with a famous satirist of the early sixties who has been pushed further and further into the margin of the culture, later and later into the reaches of the night on BBC 2, or Radio Solent, or wherever they still finally let him practise his art. He said, 'I don't understand why every day I feel my own increasing irrelevance to the country I am meant to the satirizing.' I suggested it is because satire depends upon ignorance. It is based on the proposition, 'If only you knew.' Thus the satirist can rail, 'If only you knew that Eden was on benzedrine throughout the Suez crisis, stoned out of his head and fancy-free; if only you knew that the crippled, stroke-raddled Churchill dribbled and farted in Cabinet for two years after a debilitating stroke, and nobody dared remove him; if only you knew that Cabinet Ministers sleep with tarts, that Tory MPs liaise with crooked architects and bent offshore bankers: if only you knew.' But finally after his railing, the satirist may find that the audience replies, 'Well we do know now; and we don't believe it

60

will ever change. And knowing may well not affect what we think.'

This is the first stage of what I think Marxists call 'raising consciousness'; a worthy aim and yet . . . consciousness has been raised in this country for a good many years now and we seem further from radical political change than at any time in my life. The traditional function of the radical artist - 'Look at those Borgias; look at this bureaucracy,' - has been undermined. We have looked. We have seen. We have known. And we have not changed. A pervasive cynicism paralyses public life. And the once-active, early-sixties' satirist is left on the street corner, peddling pathetic grubby little scraps of sketch and song - Callaghan's love life? Roy Jenkins' taste for claret . . . .

And so we must ask, against this background, what can the playwright accomplish that the satirist cannot? What tools does he have that the satirist lacks?

The first question a political playwright addresses himself to is: why is it that in advanced industrial societies the record of revolutionary activity is so very miserable, so very, very low? The urban proletariat in this country knows better than we ever can that they are selling their labour to capital; many of them know far better than we of the degradations of capitalism. Of the wretched and the inadequate housing into which many of them are born; of the grotesque, ever worsening imbalance in the educational system whereby the chances of progress to examinability even at 'O' level, even at CSE level, is still ludicrously low; of the functional and enslaving work they are going to have to do; of the lack of control they are going to suffer at their own workplace. Of all

these things they know far more than we, and, most
importantly, they are familiar with socialist ideas which
see their sufferings as part of a soluble political pattern.

Worse, we have lived through a time of economic
depression, which classically in Marxist theory is supposed
to throw up those critical moments at which the proletariat
may seize power. And yet, in my own estimate, European
countries have been more unstable during times of affluence
than times of depression. It is hard to believe in the
historical inevitability of something which has so
frequently not happened, or rather, often been nearest to
happening in places and circumstances furthest away from
those predicted by the man who first suggested it.

Confronted by this apparent stasis, the English writer
is inclined to answer with a stasis of his own, to sigh
and imagine that the dialectic has completely packed in,
or rather got stuck in some deep riff from which he cannot
jump it out. And so he begins to lose faith in the
possibility of any movement at all. Compare this with a
post-revolutionary society, like China, where the dialectic
is actually seen to mean something in people's lives. In
the play *Fanshen* it is dynamic. Political practice answers
to political theory and yet modifies it; the party answers
to the people and is modified by it. The fight is for
political structures which answer people's needs; and
people themselves are changed by living out theoretical
ideas. It is a story of change and progress.

Must it always be, however, that Marxist drama set in
Europe reflects the state of revolutionary politics with
an answering sluggishness of its own? By this I mean, that
sinking of the heart when you go to a political play and
find that the author really believes that certain questions

have been answered even before the play has begun. Why do
we so often have to endure the demeaning repetition of
slogans which are seen not as transitional aids to under-
standing, but as ultimate solutions to men's problems?
Why the insulting insistence in so much political theatre
that a few gimcrack mottoes of the Left will sort out the
deep problems of reaction in modern England? Why the urge
to caricature? Why the deadly stiffness of limb? Brecht
uncoils the great sleeping length of his mind to give us
in everything but the greatest of his writing exactly that
impression, the godlike feeling that the questions have
been answered before the play has begun. Even his idea
of irony is insufferably coy. He parades it, he hangs it
out to dry as if it were proof of the broadness of his
mind. It should not need such demonstration.

I do understand the thinking. The Marxist playwright
working in a fairly hostile medium, feels that his first
job is to declare his allegiance, to show his hand if you
like. He thinks that because the play itself is part of
the class struggle, an object, a weapon in that struggle,
that he must first say which side he is on and make that
clear, before he proceeds to lay out the ideas of the play
as fairly as he may. To me this approach is rubbish, it
insults the audience's intelligence; more important it
insults their experience; most important it is also a
fundamental misunderstanding of what a play is. A play
is not actors, a play is not a text; a play is what happens
between the stage and the audience. A play is a performance.
So if a play is to be a weapon in the class struggle, then
that weapon is not going to be the things you are saying; it
is the interaction of what you are saying and what the
audience is thinking. The play is in the air. The woman

63

in the balcony who yelled out during the famous performance of *Othello*, 'Can't you see what he's going to do, you stupid black fool?' expressed the life of that play better than any writer I ever knew; and understood the nature of performance better than the slaves of Marxist fashion.

I think this fact, that we are dealing, all of us, actors, writers, directors, with something we cannot calibrate because it is in the air and nowhere else, accounts for the fact that theatre is often bound up in mysticism, and why it is is known throughout the Western world as a palace of boredom. Is there any boredom like boredom in the theatre? Is there anything as grey, as soul-rotting, as nerve-tearing, as being bored in the theatre, or as facing the bleak statistical likelihood, that you will be bored in the theatre for 99 per cent of the time you spend there? I can sleep anywhere on earth, haystack, bus, railway station, I have slept soundly with mortar bombs landing eight hundred yards away, yet I cannot sleep in the theatre. This I put down to the fact that I cannot bear to sleep when so many of my fellow human beings are in such intolerable pain around me; not only my comrades in the audience, but also my colleagues on stage. For if theatre is judgement, it is also failure. It is failing, and failing, and failing.

I think that it is in some way to avoid this uncomfortable fact that dramatists have lately taken to brandishing their political credentials as frequently as possible throughout their work, and that political theatre groups have indulged in such appalling overkill, in some way to stave off failure with an audience; to flaunt your sincerity, to assert and re-assert a simple scaffolding of belief in order not to face the real and unpredictable dangers of a genuinely live performance is all a way of not being judged. It is

64

understandable, but it is wrong. It is in no way as craven as the scaffolding you will find in West End theatres, the repeated reassurances to the audience that the sick narrow lives the worst of them lead are the only lives worth leading; nor in my mind is it in any way as poisonous as the upper middle-brow, intellectual comedies which have become the snob fashion of the day, meretricious structures full of brand references to ideas at which people laugh in order to prove they have heard of them; the pianola of chic which tinkles night and day in Shaftesbury Avenue, and which is thought to be real music in the smart Sunday papers. The English theatre loves the joker, the detached observer, the man who stands outside; no wonder, faced with this ubiquity of tat, that political theatre tends to be strident and unthinking, not in its attitude to its content, but in its distrust of the essential nature of performance itself.

Historically it is hard for a serious playwright to be confident. History has not behaved in the way that was asked of it; and the medium itself in which we work has chronic doubts about its own audibility. Bronowski hectors from a corner of a tenement slum; while the Queen settles down on Fridays to watch 'It Ain't Half Hot Mum'. The airways are saturated with conflicting messages. All a playwright can do is promise to speak only when he has something to say; but when he speaks, what special role can he assume?

To try and answer I must turn to the series of choices which I have made and try to justify them. In passing, by the way, it's worth remembering how often theatre has been compared to dream; for me the analogy is clinched by the way that, as with dreams, your own are so much more interesting than anybody else's.

For five years I have been writing history plays. I
try to show the English their history. I write tribal
pieces, trying to show how people behaved on this island,
off this continental shelf, in this century. How this
Empire vanished, how these ideals died. Reading Angus
Calder's *The People's War* changed all my thinking as a
writer; an account of the Second World War through the
eyes of ordinary people, it attempts a complete alternative
history to the phoney and corrupting history I was taught
at school. Howard Brenton and I attempted in *Brassneck* to
write what I have no doubt Calder would still write far
better than we, an imagined subsequent volume *The People's
Peace*, as seen, in our case, through the lives of the petty
bourgeoisie, builders, solicitors, brewers, politicians,
the masonic gang who carve up provincial England. It was
my first step into the past. When I first wrote, I wrote
in the present day, I believed in a purely contemporary
drama; so as I headed backwards, I worried I was copping
out, avoiding the real difficulties of the day. It took
me time to realize that the reason was, if you write about
now, just today and nothing else, then you seem to be
confronting only stasis; but if you begin to describe the
movement of history, if you write plays that cover passages
of time, then you begin to find a sense of movement, of
social change, if you like; and the facile hopelessness that
comes from confronting the day and only the day, the room
and only the room, begins to disappear and in its place the
writer can offer a record of movement and change.

You will see what I am arguing. The Marxist writer spends
a great deal of time rebuking societies for not behaving in
the way that he expected them to; but also, furious because
66

change is not taking the form he would like it to, he denigrates or ignores the real changes which have taken place in the last thirty years. A great Empire falls apart, offering, as it collapses, a last great wash of wealth through this country, unearned, unpaid for, a shudder of plenty, which has dissolved so many of the rules which kept the game in order; while intellectuals grope wildly for an answer, any answer to the moral challenge of collectivism, the citizens have spent and spent, after the war in a time of wealth, but recently in a time of encroaching impoverishment. We are living through a great, groaning, yawling festival of change - but because this is England it is not always seen on the streets. In my view it is seen in the extraordinary intensity of peoples' personal despair, and it is to that despair that as a historical writer I choose to address myself time and time again: in *Teeth 'n' Smiles,* in *Knuckle,* in *Plenty.*

I feel exactly as Tom Wolfe does in a marvellous account of his opportunism as a writer, 'About the time I came to New York . . . the most serious novelists had abandoned the richest terrain of the novel: namely, society, the social tableau, manners and morals, the whole business of the "way we live now". There is no novelist who captures the Sixties in America or even in New York in the sense that Thackeray was the chronicler of London in the 1840s and Balzac was the chronicler of Paris and all of France . . . . That was marvellous for journalists, I tell you that. The Sixties were one of the most extraordinary decades in American history in terms of manners and morals. Manners and morals *were* history in the Sixties. I couldn't believe the scene I saw spread out before me. But what really amazed

me as a writer I had it practically all to myself . . . .
As fast as I could possibly do it, I was turning out
articles on this amazing spectacle I saw bubbling and
screaming right there . . . and all the while I knew that
some enterprising novelist was going to come along and DO
the whole marvellous scene in one gigantic daring bold
stroke. It was so ready, so ripe - beckoning . . .
and it never happened.'

I can't tell you how accurately that expresses a
feeling I have always had as a playwright and which I know
colleagues have experienced, that sense that the greater
part of the culture is simply looking at the wrong things.
I became a writer by default, to fill in the gaps, to
work on areas of the fresco which were simply ignored, or
appropriated for the shallowest purposes: rock music, black
propaganda, gun-selling, diplomacy. And yet I cannot
believe to this day, that a much more talented writer will
not come along and DO the whole scene. In common with
other writers who look with their eyes, I have been abused
in newspapers for being hysterical, strident and obscene,
when all I was doing was observing the passing scene, its
stridency, its hysteria, its obscenity, and trying to put
it in a historical context which the literary community
seems pathologically incapable of contemplating. In
Teeth 'n' Smiles a girl chooses to go to prison because
it will give her an experience of suffering which is
bound in her eyes to be more worthwhile than the life
she could lead outside: not one English critic could
bring himself to mention this central event in the play,
its plausibility, its implications. It was beyond their
scope to engage with such an idea. And yet, how many
people here have close friends who have taken control of
68

their own lives, only to destroy them?

We are drawing close, I think to what I hope a playwright can do. He can put people's sufferings in a historical context; and by doing that, he can help to explain their pain. But what I mean by history will not be the mechanized absolving force theorists would like it to be; it will be those strange uneasy factors that make a place here and nowhere else, make a time now and no other time. A theatre which is exclusively personal, just a place of private psychology is inclined to self-indulgence; a theatre which is just social is inclined to unreality, to the impatient blindness I've talked about today. Yeats said, out of our quarrel with others, we make rhetoric, while out of our quarrel with ourselves, we make poetry. I value both, and value the theatre as a place where both are given weight.

I write love stories. Most of my plays are that. Over and over again I have written about romantic love, because it never goes away. And the view of the world it provides, the dislocation it offers, is the most intense experience that many people know on earth.

And I write comedy because . . . such ideas as the one I have just uttered make me laugh.

And I write about politics because the challenge of communism, in however debased and ugly a form, is to ask whether the criteria by which we have brought up are right; whether what each of us experiences uniquely really is what makes us valuable; whether every man should really be his own cocktail; or whether our criteria could and should be collective, and if they were, whether we would be any happier. However absolute the sufferings of men in the totalitarian Soviet countries, however decadent the current

69

life of the West, the fact is that this question has only just been asked, and we have not even the first hundredth of an answer. To give up now would be death.

I said at the beginning that I have chosen to speak, in part simply to find out, to put my ear to the ground. And I must tell you what I find in universities. I find a generation who are cowed, who seem to have given up on the possibility of change, who seem to think that most of the experiments you could make with the human spirit are likely to be doomed or at any rate highly embarrassing. There is a demeaning nostalgia for the radicalism of the late sixties, people wanting to know exactly what the Vietnam marches were like. To me it would be sad if a whole generation's lives were shaped by the fact that a belief in change had fallen temporarily out of fashion; in Tom Wolfe's terms, it would be sad if this historical period had no chroniclers.

Our lives must be refreshed with images which are not official, not approved; that break what Orwell called 'the Geneva conventions of the mind'. These images may come on television, something of a poisoned well in my view, because of its preference for censoring its own best work, or simply banning it; or they may come in this unique arena of judgement, the theatre.

When I look back on 1978 it will not be Callaghan's face that I shall want to remember; the bleak logistics of his world will evoke very little to me, I am sure. Instead, I shall perhaps remember a tramp stretched across three seats in the warm, on the Victoria line, fast asleep his right hand gently cradling his cock, while the rest of us in the carriage stared impassively ahead. What historical forces drew him there? What armies fought?

What families fell apart? What compensating impulse guides his hand?

I find it strange to theorize. Mostly theatre is hard work and nothing else. It is no coincidence that some of the British theatre's loudest theorists are notoriously incompetent inside a rehearsal room. It is a different kind of work. The patterns that I've made today in my own work and talking about others are purely retrospective, just the afterbirth; the wonder of performance is - you will always be surprised. The short, angry, sandy-haired, squat playwright turns out to write plays which *you* experience as slow, langorous, relaxed and elegant: the great night you had in the theatre two years ago turns out upon re-reading to be a piece of stinking fish. I would wish it no other way.

An old American vaudevillian of the thirties drank his career away, fell into universal disfavour, but was finally found and put into an old people's home in California by a kindly producer who had once worked with him many years before. Visiting the old actor on his deathbed, the producer said, 'You are facing death. Is it as people describe? Is there a final sense of reassurance, a feeling of resignation, that sense of letting go that writers tell us consoles the dying?' 'Not at all,' said the comic 'on the contrary. Death is none of those things, that I was promised. It is ugly and fierce and degrading and violent. It is hard,' he said, 'hard as playing comedy.' All I would add is, not as hard as writing it.